THE NEED TO KNOW LIBRARY™

EVERYTHING YOU NEED TO KNOW ABOUT

BIRTH CONTROL

ALANA BENSON

Rosen
YA™

New York

Published in 2019 by The Rosen Publishing Group, Inc.
29 East 21st Street, New York, NY 10010

Library of Congress Cataloging-in-Publication Data

Names: Benson, Alana, author.
Title: Everything you need to know about birth control / Alana Benson.
Description: New York : Rosen YA, 2019. | Series: The need to know library |
Includes bibliographical references and index. | Audience: Grades 7–12.
Identifiers: LCCN 2018003829| ISBN 9781508183433 (library bound) | ISBN 9781508183426 (pbk.)
Subjects: LCSH: Contraception—Juvenile literature.
Classification: LCC RG136.3 .B46 2019 | DDC 613.9/4—dc23
LC record available at https://lccn.loc.gov/2018003829

Manufactured in the United States of America

ABOUT THE AUTHOR

Alana Benson has worked with kids and teens in schools and in multiple after-school programs. She has seen firsthand the effects of poor sex education on communities, and she believes in a future where women can get the information they need—without judgment. She has written three other books, two on the topic of identity theft, and a book for Rosen Publishing on crack and cocaine abuse.

PHOTO CREDITS

CONTENTS

INTRODUCTION

Learning about birth control can be intimidating. Even asking about birth control can feel embarrassing or awkward. If you don't have an adult you can trust in your life, it probably means you're getting your information from your friends or the internet. The internet is a great resource if you're looking at the right stuff. Unfortunately, there is also some really bad information out there, especially when it comes to sex and birth control.

So why do people use birth control anyway? Primarily, it's a way to prevent pregnancy. Some forms of birth control, such as condoms, also provide protection against sexually transmitted diseases, or STDs, but not all types of birth control protect against STDs. Because of this, many people use two forms of birth control—for example, birth control pills and condoms—to protect against not only pregnancy but STDs as well. There are other reasons people may use certain forms of birth control, such as reducing acne or making periods more manageable.

When it comes to birth control, sex is inherently part of the conversation. The main reason people use birth control is so they can have sex while preventing pregnancy. Most often when people choose to have sex, it's because they enjoy sex, not because they want to have a baby. Birth control is still a controversial topic for

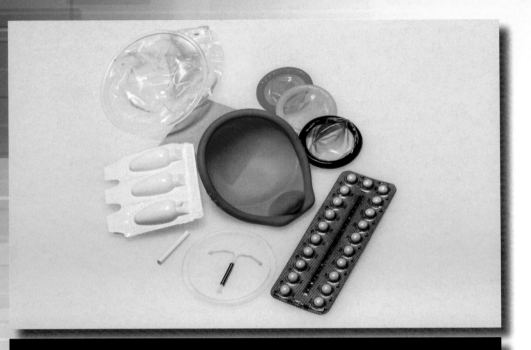

There are lots of different forms of birth control. These include physical barriers, such as condoms, and pills that work with your body's hormones to prevent a pregnancy.

some people, but learning more about it can help you decide where your beliefs lie. Knowing about birth control will help you understand some important political discussions, such as the debates around health care, insurance, and even abortion. You may not be too worried about insurance or health care today, but it is useful to understand how birth control can be a part of a much bigger conversation.

Whatever you choose to do with your life, you should know that having sex does not make you a bad or immoral person, and not having sex does not make you a prude. The choice about whether or not to have sex is yours and yours alone. You should never be pressured into having sex or pressure someone else into sex. Sex is intimate, and for most people, it is something they prefer to keep private. When it comes to sex, having a partner whom you trust is important, especially when it comes to birth control. If you and your partner can't have an open discussion about how you are going to protect yourselves from STDs and getting pregnant, you may not be ready to have sex in the first place.

Learning about birth control can put you in control of your future, whether you are female, male, or nonbinary. Even if you can't get pregnant yourself, you still need to take responsibility for birth control. Anyone who can become pregnant or who is having sex with someone who can become pregnant needs to know about birth control. This knowledge can empower you to make choices that will keep you in school, on track, and generally happy and healthy.

CHAPTER ONE

A BRIEF HISTORY OF BIRTH CONTROL

According to Jonathan Eig, author of *The Birth of the Pill: How Four Crusaders Reinvented Sex and Launched a Revolution*, "For as long as men and women have been making babies, they've been trying not to." Long before the birth control pill (sometimes called just the Pill) was invented, people tried to figure out ways to prevent pregnancy. As early as 3000 BCE, people used linen cloth, animal intestines, and even fish bladders as condoms, or physical barriers between two people having sex. In ancient Egypt, circa 1500 BCE, women would make a paste out of crocodile dung to insert inside themselves before having sex. Ancient China saw women drinking lead and mercury to prevent pregnancy, and the Greek doctor Soranus advised women to hold their breath and to try to sneeze after sex to prevent pregnancy.

Birth control has come a long way since then, and modern forms of contraception include condoms, the Pill, and a number of other hormonal and nonhormonal methods, many of which are very effective at preventing pregnancy when used correctly. However, since the

Gum arabic, produced by the acacia shrub, was used as a contraceptive in ancient Egypt.

nineteenth century, there has been vocal opposition to birth control from religious groups propagating the idea that birth control leads to immorality. These groups often have influence over politicians, and, as a result, access to birth control still faces legal challenges.

ANTHONY COMSTOCK VS. MARGARET SANGER

Although sex (especially for women) had been viewed as scandalous for some time, it wasn't until 1873 that conservative views about birth control started influencing policy in the United States. Anthony Comstock was a postal investigator who believed that the world around him was crumbling into an obscene, immoral mess. Utilizing an 1865 law that made it illegal to send "obscene" books, pamphlets, or pictures through the mail (originally created to keep Civil War soldiers from sending and receiving racy material), Comstock lobbied for

Margaret Sanger was an early advocate for birth control and had no tolerance for Anthony Comstock's censorship of family-planning newsletters and pamphlets.

drugs or medicines to be added to the list. The Comstock Act of 1873 made it so that birth control, and even information about birth control, could not be widely distributed.

One woman who clashed with Comstock was Margaret Sanger, a strong advocate for women's rights to plan their families and futures. As a nurse, she saw firsthand how devastating an unwanted pregnancy could be. She saw women who had resorted to back-alley abortions and women already living in poverty, desperate not to have another child. Sanger pioneered the

WHO CAN GET PREGNANT ANYWAY?

Many people assume that only women and girls can get pregnant and have babies, but the truth is more complicated than that. In fact, anyone with the reproductive parts to accommodate a baby (including ovaries and a uterus) may be able to get pregnant. While these people are usually assigned female at birth, that doesn't mean that they all identify as women. Some transgender men and nonbinary individuals who have ovaries and uteruses choose to get pregnant, give birth, and even breastfeed or chestfeed (a term for nursing used by some trans men and nonbinary people who do not identify as having breasts). When thinking about sex, bodies, and birth control, it's important to remember that gender identity is not the same as biological sex. So not everyone who takes the Pill or uses an IUD is a woman, and not everyone who wears a condom on their penis is a man or a boy.

birth control and sex education movements as we know them. She even coined the phrase "birth control" in her monthly newsletter, *The Woman Rebel*, a publication in direct violation of Comstock's beloved obscenity law.

In 1916, Sanger opened the first family-planning clinic in the United States, which was shut down within a week. Her advocacy led to a 1938 trial that resulted in the legalization of birth control. During her lifetime, she also underwrote the research for the first-ever birth control pill, saw

Having a baby is a lifelong commitment. Using birth control can help you plan to start a family when you're ready or prevent a pregnancy if you decide having kids isn't for you.

its approval by the FDA, and formed the organization that would later become Planned Parenthood. Sanger believed that, "Birth control is the first important step woman must take toward the goal of her freedom. It is the first step she must take to be man's equal. It is the first step they must both take toward human emancipation."

BIRTH CONTROL AND THE LAW

Legalization of contraception (another word for birth control) did not happen overnight, and neither did the scientific innovations that allowed it. The methods of birth control that are commonplace today underwent long clinical studies and trials to make sure they were safe. The feminist movement impacted these innovations, as women called for both safer birth control and better access to it. In 1970, women protested a version of oral contraception (the Pill) that was unsafe. Legislation changed, and a safer version was produced. The IUD has gone through similar developments, with activists protesting unsafe versions of the IUD and demanding safer alternatives.

Birth control is not the only thing that has changed. One landmark court case, *Roe v. Wade*, completely changed the way abortions were handled. After a Texas woman, anonymously called Jane Roe, was blocked from getting an abortion, her court case was taken all the way to the Supreme Court, where the justices decided that blocking access to abortions was unconstitutional. This 1973 court decision was revolutionary, but it certainly didn't solve everything. Today, abortion is still a controversial topic for many people, and the right to abortion continues to face legal challenges on a regular basis.

WHY DOES BIRTH CONTROL MATTER?

If the history of birth control illustrates anything, it's that people will sometimes go to crazy lengths to avoid getting pregnant, except, in many cases, stop having sex. So why does having access to birth control matter? To answer this, consider all the different ways unplanned pregnancies affect people around the world.

Many people have babies before they are ready to become parents. According to the United Nations' 2017 Revision of World Population Prospects, a quarter of the women in the world live in countries where the average age a woman has her first child is younger than twenty. On average, women who have children at a younger age are less likely to get an education, more likely to have more children, and less able to provide for those children.

According to the Guttmacher Institute, roughly 222 million women globally cannot get access to birth

The more children a person has, the more time and money it takes to feed them, clothe them, take them to the doctor, and send them to school.

control. For these women, not being able to plan their families puts them at risk in multiple ways. Getting pregnant later in life comes with multiple health complications and can be dangerous for both the pregnant person and the child. Having babies that are closely spaced does not allow a person's body time to properly heal between pregnancies. It can be overwhelming to wade through the maze of abortion options, and in many countries, abortion is not even legal. This leads people to seek back-alley abortions. Each year about sixty-eight thousand pregnant people die as a result of unsafe abortions.

With access to birth control, women are able to plan their lives, stay in school, and take care of the children they actually want to have. Moreover, access to birth control doesn't just affect individuals—it creates change on a gigantic scale. According to a 2015 estimate by Planned Parenthood, for every $1 invested in family planning programs, federal and state governments save $7.09. Access to birth control reduces abortions, teen pregnancies, and unintended pregnancies, leading to healthier and happier families.

MYTHS AND FACTS

MYTH: I'm a bad person for having sex.

FACT: Not even close! As long as you and your partner both want to have sex, you both feel ready, and you both know where you stand about your feelings (whether you're just having fun or in a committed relationship), having sex is a perfectly normal thing to do. However, sex does come with a lot of responsibilities, like using protection and communicating honestly with your partner.

MYTH: If I use any form of birth control, I'm totally fine.

FACT: Some forms of birth control are more effective (meaning you are less likely to get pregnant) than others. Using condoms, for example, is much safer than using the "pull-out" method. Any method is better than no method, but it's important to follow the exact instructions for whichever method(s) of birth control you use to make sure it's as effective as possible.

MYTH: All forms of birth control protect against STDs.

FACT: Definitely not true. Only one form, condoms, does protect against STDs, though it is not 100 percent foolproof. If the condom tears or is not put on correctly, you can still be exposed to STDs. The only way to be sure you don't have an STD is to get tested.

CHAPTER TWO

HORMONAL METHODS

To understand how birth control works, you have to understand how getting pregnant works in the first place. In order to get pregnant, a person must be ovulating. Ovulation is the time when the body releases an egg from the ovary into the fallopian tube. These tubes carry the egg to the uterus. If there are no sperm waiting in the fallopian tube to fertilize the egg, a pregnancy cannot occur. There is a catch: while an unfertilized egg can live for only twenty-four hours, sperm can live up to six days. This means if two people have sex days before ovulation, the ovulating person could still get pregnant.

HORMONES: THE GOOD, THE BAD, AND THE UGLY

Hormonal birth control works by suppressing ovulation with hormones, the chemical messengers in the body that control bodily functions. Hormonal methods can be very effective in preventing pregnancy, and

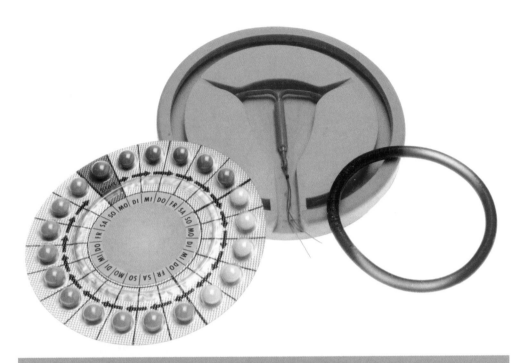

Hormonal birth control methods, like some IUDs, the ring, and birth control pills, work well for some people, while others may experience severe side effects.

many people use these methods without side effects. However, others have a tough time adjusting to the additional hormones in their bodies. Learning about each type can help you choose the birth control that is right for you and your body.

Hormonal forms of birth control, while highly effective, can cause problems, especially later in life. People who have used hormonal birth control for much of their lives can have a tougher time navigating menopause (the transition from being fertile and having your menstrual period to the end of your body's reproductive period). Think about it: if your body has been relying on hormones from a different source, it can become a problem once it has to rely on its own. Hormonal birth control has been linked to depression, weight gain, and a drastically lowered sex drive. This is not to say that hormonal birth control is not a good option, but that you should carefully consider what method you should take by learning about your family's medical history and talking honestly with a doctor about your options.

BIRTH CONTROL PILLS

When most people hear the words "birth control," they think of the birth control pill, also known as the Pill. There are two main types of pills and lots of different brands. The two distinct kinds are combination pills and progestin-only pills. Combination pills use a combination of two hormones, estrogen and progestin, to keep the ovaries from releasing an egg. No egg means no pregnancy. These hormones also work together to thin the lining of the uterus (making it harder for a fertilized egg to attach after it reached the uterus) and thicken cervical mucus (to make it harder for the sperm to move). Combination pills have added benefits, like helping you to have lighter, more comfortable periods, clearing up acne, and even reducing the risk of ovarian and endometrial cancer, though some studies link it to a higher risk for breast cancer.

You should not use the combination pill if you have high blood pressure or if you smoke and are over thirty-five. Since combination pills contain estrogen, they can have side effects like breast tenderness, nausea, and mood swings, though these side effects can vary from person to person. Some people may not experience any side effects, while others may experience a lot.

Most combination pills come in twenty-eight-day pill packs. The last week is made up of inactive or placebo pills (which sometimes have vitamins in them to help stabilize your body during the week of your period). This is the week you'll have your period. Progestin-only pills (also called the minipill) sometimes suppress ovulation, but the main way they work is to thicken cervical mucus. If you suffer from the side effects of the combination pill, your doctor might prescribe progestin-only pills. Progestin-only pills do not have inactive pills, so you have to take the pills every day for them to be effective.

With perfect use, birth control pills are 99 percent effective. How do you use birth control pills perfectly? Take them every day at the same time (or within two hours—so if you take them at 9:00 a.m. one day, take them before 11:00 a.m. the next day), and don't skip days. If you start skipping pills or taking them at different times, their effectiveness can drop down to 91 percent. Most people who get pregnant while taking birth control pills are not taking them perfectly. To help you take these pills in the correct way, set a reminder for yourself on your phone and put them next to something you use every day, like your toothbrush.

Some types of medication can also make the Pill less effective, so make sure you talk to your doctor about any medication you take.

HORMONAL IUDS

The IUD, or intrauterine device, is more than 99 percent effective, making it one of the most effective forms of birth control. A hormonal IUD is a small, T-shaped piece of plastic that sits just inside the uterus and uses the hormone progestin (just like the Pill) to thicken cervical mucus and prevent sperm from fertilizing eggs. Having the IUD inserted may be painful. Doctors say it will feel like a menstrual cramp, but many people say it ranges from a pinch to an intense pain. That moment of pain, however, can give you between three and six years of

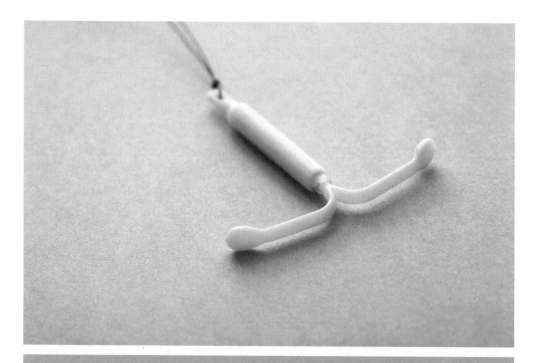

The thought of having an IUD inside your body may seem intimidating. Don't worry, though. Once an IUD is in place, most people can't feel it.

99 percent protection from pregnancy. The IUD is mostly maintenance free—you don't have to remember to do something every day. Aside from checking occasionally to make sure the strings of the IUD are in the right place (your doctor can show you how when you have it inserted), you can get it and forget it. Because there is no room for human error—there is no perfect use when it comes to an IUD—you can't mess it up to reduce your odds.

There are four hormonal brands of IUD: Mirena, Skyla, Liletta, and Kyleena. Each of these varies in how long it can stay in, but with each one, you can get pregnant shortly after you have it removed. Just like every method of birth control, IUDs have their own list of side

WHAT DO RABBITS AND YAMS HAVE TO DO WITH IT?

Scientists discovered progesterone—a hormone in birth control—in rabbits! Scientists worried about the expense of extractig the hormone from rabbits, and others worried about it being inhumane. Luckily, a researcher named Russell Marker found progesterone in a Mexican yam called cabeza de negro. By extracting the hormone from a plant instead of from an animal, the process became less expensive and more humane. It also allowed birth control to be produced in mass quantities faster. That meant more people could have access to more birth control. What do you know, birth control from yams!

effects. Hormonal IUDs can lead to lighter periods and even reduce cramps, but they can increase the amount of spotting you have in between periods. The more serious side effects include infection and the IUD slipping out of place, and in some rare cases, pushing through the wall of the uterus. To avoid this, check your IUD strings regularly, or have your doctor check once a year to be sure the IUD is sitting right where it should be.

OTHER HORMONAL METHODS

There are other forms of hormonal birth control. One is the implant, a metal rod that is inserted into the skin of your upper arm. It's about the size of a match, and like the IUD, it's a maintenance-free method. Since there is no room for human error, it is 99 percent effective. It works for four years by preventing sperm from getting to the egg with hormones. There is also a hormonal injection, known as Depo-Provera. You need to go to your doctor and get the shot every three months for this method to be effective.

If you don't like the idea of something being inserted or injected into your body, there is the patch. The patch is exactly what it sounds like. It's a small piece of sticky fabric (like a square Band-Aid) that you keep on your body for a week at a time. The patch releases hormones that can prevent pregnancy. You change the patch every week, and don't wear one on the week of your period. With perfect use, the patch is 99 percent effective. With typical use, like forgetting to put a new patch on, it drops to 91 percent, just like the birth control pill.

There is also the Nuvaring, a small, hormonal ring that you (no trip to the doctor required!) insert inside your vagina every month. It's a lot like putting in a tampon. The ring has a lower dose of hormones, so if other hormonal methods mess with your body too much, the ring might be a good option.

SIDE EFFECTS

While hormones work well for many people, they can be hard to adjust to. Possible side effects of hormonal birth control include spotting (bleeding in between

Nausea can be a side effect of hormonal birth control. If hormonal methods don't work for you, there are lots of other options.

periods), breast tenderness, nausea, increased vaginal discharge, a change in sex drive, clearing up acne, making acne worse, making periods easier, and making periods harder to handle. Some people may experience depression, headaches, irregular periods, anxiety, and hair loss or gain. If you find a method that works well for you, that's awesome! If you need help remembering to change your patch, take your pill, or remove your Nuvaring, write it down in a calendar or set alerts on your phone to help you take your birth control perfectly and not just typically.

You won't really know how a method of birth control affects your body until you try it. Birth control has come a long way since Margaret Sanger's days, but unfortunately people still have to deal with a lot in order to not get pregnant. The bottom line is that your body is unique, and even if your mom or your friend or your doctor thinks a particular method will work for you, you won't know until you try it yourself.

It's also important not to get discouraged. Pills make you feel crazy? Get off them and try something else. Preventing an unwanted pregnancy is super important, but so is feeling good in your day-to-day life. Also, none of these methods protect against STDs, so it's always a good idea to use a condom as a backup, or get a check-up with your partner (if you two are monogamous) to make sure you are both STD free.

CHAPTER THREE

NONHORMONAL AND BARRIER METHODS

F or some people, the side effects of hormonal birth control make it impossible to live a happy day-to-day life. Others are concerned about what a lifetime of hormones will do when they stop taking birth control and enter menopause. Still others just don't like the idea of messing with their body chemistry. For these people (and maybe you're one of them) there are still plenty of other birth control options.

Keep in mind that, while eliminating hormones lessens the side effects for most people, that doesn't mean that all the nonhormonal methods will work perfectly for you. Finding the right birth control is like a game of elimination: you just have to find the one that works for you as an individual.

COPPER IUD

The copper IUD, called ParaGard, is the only nonhormonal IUD. The copper produces an inflammatory reaction in the uterus that kills sperm. The copper IUD can also stay in the uterus for ten years! That is ten years of 99 percent effective birth control. The copper IUD can cause worse periods, though, with more severe cramping, than the other IUDs. It also comes with the same raft of side effects, depending on the individual. Some people have even experienced swollen lymph nodes because of it.

CONDOMS

Condoms may be the most popular form of birth control. Condoms create a physical barrier between you and your partner, which is how they protect against STDs. They

Condoms are one of the most common barrier methods, and one of the only birth control methods that also protects against STDs.

have no hormones or side effects, require no prescription or doctor visits, and you can buy them just about everywhere. Condoms are also the only birth control method that protects against STDs, so many people use them in addition to another method of birth control.

Condoms have to be used every single time you have sex. Be aware that they can break, leaving you at risk for an unintended pregnancy or STD. Condoms can degrade, so be sure to check the expiration date. There are lots of different kinds of condoms, and it's important that they fit correctly. If you or your partner has a latex allergy, nonlatex condom options are available.

External condoms, often called male condoms, are rolled onto the penis, with a half-inch (1.3 centimeters) of extra space at the top. This extra space ensures the semen has a place to go after orgasm. There shouldn't be any air bubbles, as they can cause condoms to break. Condoms should always be thrown away after use, and never used twice. Using two condoms at the same time does not make them more effective. In fact, it makes them more likely to break.

Internal condoms, often called female condoms, work in a similar fashion, just on the inside of a vagina rather than the outside of a penis. The remainder of the condom should be on the outside of the vagina, to protect the vulva from contact. You can even insert one up to six hours before you have sex, so you don't have to worry about it in the moment. Just like external condoms, internal condoms should never be used more than once, they should be used every single time you have sex, and if they break, they are no longer effective.

It's a good idea to use lubrication with both types of condoms. The latex or other materials in condoms can have a drying effect and make for an unpleasant experience. Using lube will help you and your partner have an easier, more enjoyable time and help to prevent the condom from breaking. Note that oil-based lubricants can damage condoms and make them less effective, so you should only use silicone-based or water-based lube with condoms.

OTHER BARRIER METHODS

Cervical caps and diaphragms are inserted into the vagina to cover the cervix so that sperm is blocked.

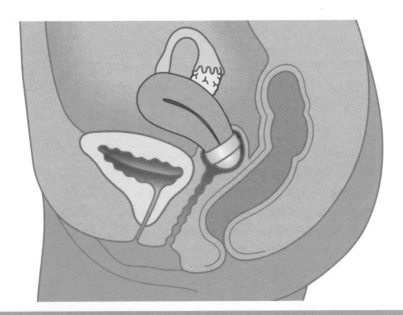

Cervical caps (illustrated by the little white cup) sit right over the cervix to serve as a barrier to the uterus.

These barrier methods are a little trickier to use and have a higher failure rate than other types of birth control. You should use spermicide with both of these methods to make them more effective. Spermicides are chemical creams inserted into the vagina that stop sperm from getting to the egg. Spermicides can be used with condoms as well.

A BRIEF HISTORY OF FORCED STERILIZATION

Forced sterilization has been used throughout history as a means of controlling people who were seen as "unfit" to have children. These groups included people with disabilities, people of color, poor people, unmarried mothers, convicted criminals, and sex workers. By controlling minority populations, people in power have sought to cease the reproductive cycles of groups they did not like or were afraid of.

Forced sterilization was popular with people who believed in eugenics, a set of beliefs that promotes selective breeding as a means to "improve" humanity. Eugenics was popularized in Nazi Germany as a way of justifying the murder of millions of people. Margaret Sanger, the mother of birth control, has been widely criticized for her support of eugenics programs.

Forced sterilization has occurred widely in the United States as recently as the 1960s and '70s. According to a study by the US General Accounting Office, 3,406 Native American women were sterilized without permission between 1973 and 1976. From 2006 to 2010, almost 150 female prisoners were forcibly sterilized in California.

Cervical caps and diaphragms have a failure rate of 14 to 29 percent, which is pretty high. They also have to be inserted every time before sex in order to be effective, and the cervical cap has to be fitted by a doctor to ensure it will fit you properly.

STERILIZATION

If you are 100 percent certain you do not want to have biological children, there are permanent birth control options. Sterilization is surgery that permanently makes a person infertile. Cisgender women and other people

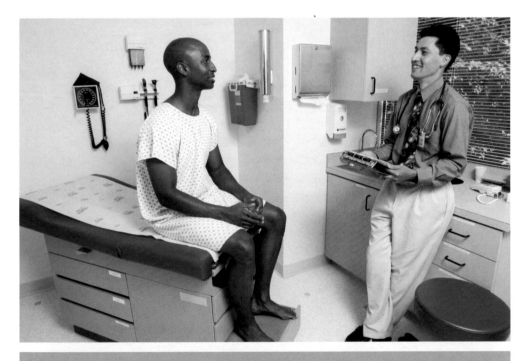

Cisgender men and other people who produce sperm may choose to have a sterilization operation known as a vasectomy if they are sure they don't want to have children or more children than they have.

with uteruses who do not want to have children can have tubal ligation, more commonly known as "getting your tubes tied." Tubal ligation blocks the fallopian tubes, so sperm cannot meet the egg to fertilize it. The procedure involves anesthesia, and the recovery time can vary from a few days to a week. There is also a nonsurgical option, known as fallopian tube occlusion or Essure, but it takes three months to become effective.

There is also a sterilization surgery for cisgender men and other people who produce sperm. A vasectomy is a twenty-minute procedure that permanently blocks sperm from entering the seminal fluid. After this procedure, you need to return to your doctor to have your sperm tested before you can safely have sex without getting your partner pregnant.

It is possible to reverse some kinds of sterilization surgeries, but the reversal is not always successful. Don't forget, even if you have had sterilization surgery, you still need to use condoms to protect against STDs.

CHAPTER FOUR

NATURAL METHODS

S ide effects of birth control can range from mild to life altering. This is why some people opt for natural methods. Some people don't like the idea of adding anything to their body chemistry, and others may just not be interested in any of the other methods.

FERTILITY AWARENESS AND TRACKING

Fertility awareness and tracking focuses on a person's monthly menstrual cycle, figuring out which days ovulation (and thus fertility) occur, and avoiding sex or using protection on those days. People who menstruate have been tracking their cycles for thousands of years, in their own ways. Keeping a careful eye on your cycle can help you avoid getting pregnant. While cycle tracking can be as low as 70 percent effective with typical use, tracking your period can help you get to know your body better in lots of other ways. Many people track their period just to better understand how their body works and to know when to expect their period

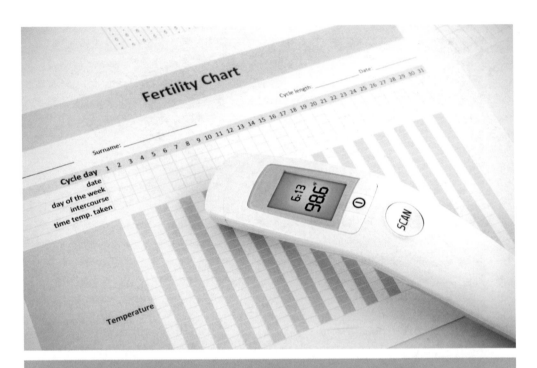

Fertility tracking has no side effects, but it does require diligence to keep up with the routine. It will, however, help you get in tune with your body's natural rhythm.

and premenstrual syndrome, or PMS. The pros of fertility tracking include that it has no side effects and involves no doctor visits, but the cons include a low level of effectiveness.

WITHDRAWAL

Withdrawal, or the "pull-out" method, requires a person to remove their penis from their partner before they ejaculate. Withdrawal requires major self-control on the part of the person with the penis and a lot of trust from

THERE'S AN APP FOR THAT

Not sold on a metal implant or a daily pill? There's an app for that! Developed by Swedish nuclear physicist and Nobel Prize winner Elina Berglund, the Natural Cycles app uses an algorithm to help people who menstruate know when they are fertile. Natural Cycles is the only certified app for contraception. App users take their temperature every day and log it in the app. Using the app is similar to tracking your fertility on a calendar, the way people have been doing for thousands of years, except it's a little more high-tech and a lot more accurate. The app tells you whether or not you are fertile that day, and thus whether you can safely have sex without getting pregnant, or whether you should abstain or use protection. On green days, you can safely have sex without getting pregnant. On red days, you can't.

Just like every other form of birth control (aside from the IUD), there are factors that make it more and less effective. When the app is used perfectly, there is only a five-in-one-thousand chance of becoming pregnant, which is similar to the effectiveness of the Pill. However, when it is used imperfectly (for example, if users don't use protection on red days or forget to take their temperature), that figure drops to a seven-in-one-hundred chance of getting pregnant.

Taking your temperature every day and abstaining or using protection on fertile days requires a lot of diligence. This method is best for individuals who are responsible and organized or for those who have experienced negative side effects from other forms of birth control. The app costs $80 a year, making it a good alternative if you don't

If you use the fertility tracking method, you will use a thermometer first thing in the morning, every day, to figure out where you are in your cycle and whether or not you may be fertile.

have health insurance. Since you are not putting anything new into your body, it has no side effects. This form of birth control doesn't protect against STDs.

their partner. While this might be the oldest form of birth control, it does have a 22 percent failure rate. If you do not have total self-control or you are not careful to keep semen away from the vulva, your partner can still get pregnant. This method does not require a prescription, and it can be used with another method to make it more effective. It does not, however, prevent STDs.

WHERE THEM BOYS AT?

Traditionally, birth control has been seen as the responsibility of the person who can get pregnant—usually the woman. This is no accident. In the beginning, Margaret Sanger believed that women needed to be in control of their bodies and thus in control of birth control. Over the years, there have been several attempts to market "male" birth control pills, shots, and other methods. So where are they now? The majority of them were discontinued because "the risks to the study participants outweighed the potential benefits," according an independent committee quoted by Julie Beck in the *Atlantic*. What were those risks? Mood changes, depression, pain at the injection site, and increased libido.

All of those side effects are commonplace for women on FDA-approved birth control. The IUD can perforate the uterus (in very rare cases), but it is still approved for women to use. The undeniable thread is that for people with uteruses, birth control has been revolutionary. For people who can't get pregnant themselves, the stakes are much lower. They don't have to worry about carrying a baby for nine months and giving birth, and they are unlikely to have to quit their careers or stop going to school in order to care for a child. People with uteruses will generally choose the side effects over not getting pregnant, whereas when it comes to cisgender men, those side effects are deemed unacceptable before the birth control even hits the market.

ABSTINENCE

Abstinence means abstaining from sex (at least, the kind of sex that involves a penis penetrating a vagina), and it is the only 100 percent effective method for preventing pregnancy. The only problem with abstinence is it means you can't have intercourse. If you have no interest in this kind of sex, that's fine. You are pretty much guaranteed not to get pregnant. However, abstinence can be difficult to maintain. If you are in a relationship, make sure you and your partner are on the same page as to what kinds of sexual activity you

Studies show that teens who have access to factual information about sex and how to prevent pregnancy are less likely to become pregnant before they're ready.

want to engage in. Abstinence from intercourse doesn't mean you can't be sexual together in other ways.

While abstinence works well in theory, a 2011 study found that abstinence education in the United States does not cause teens to abstain from having sex. According to a report by Kathrin Stanger-Hall and David Hall, "teens in states that prescribe more abstinence education are actually more likely to become pregnant." If teenagers do not have the information they need about how to prevent pregnancy, and they choose to have sex anyway, they are more likely to get pregnant.

CHAPTER FIVE

TOO LATE FOR BIRTH CONTROL?

So you had sex, and maybe you forgot to use a condom, or forgot to take the Pill. Now what? If you can, talk to your partner about it. What would

Finding out that you are pregnant when you don't want to be can be terrifying, but remember that you are not alone in this and that you have multiple options.

it be like for the two of you to raise a child? Can you afford to raise a kid? Do you want to? If you don't feel comfortable talking to your partner, look for support elsewhere, whether from a parent, a friend you trust, a counselor, or a health care provider. In the end, the decision about what to do is yours and yours alone.

EMERGENCY CONTRACEPTION

The morning-after pill is a form of emergency contraception. (The important word here is "emergency"! This form of birth control should not be used regularly because it is not as effective as other forms of birth control.) Emergency contraception stops a pregnancy before it starts. There are several pills on the market that you can take, and you can also have the copper IUD (ParaGard) inserted up to five days after having unprotected sex. This will stop a pregnancy from occurring 99.9 percent of the time, in addition to protecting you for the next ten years from having it happen again.

Morning-after pills have many of the same hormones that birth control pills have, just in higher amounts. Plan B One-Step, Next Choice One Dose, and My Way are all different variations of the morning-after pill. Some pills are taken in one dose, while others contain two pills that you take twelve hours apart.

Be sure to read all the information on the package and talk to your doctor to make sure it won't have side effects based on your medical history. Morning-after pills are more effective the sooner you take them after having

If you are pregnant, talk to your doctor about your options. Make sure you have all the information before you make any kind of decision.

unprotected sex. Many morning-after pills give you an upset stomach and may even cause you to vomit. If you do vomit, the pill may not work. Breast tenderness, irregular bleeding, dizziness, and headaches are all common side effects, but if you are worried or if those symptoms do not go away after twenty-four hours, call your doctor.

ABORTION

If you find out that you are pregnant and you don't want to have the baby, you may be considering having an

PRO-LIFE VS. PRO-CHOICE

Abortion is a controversial topic in the United States. Some people believe it should be illegal while others believe it is a fundamental human right. According to a 2015 Gallup poll, 50 percent of Americans identified as pro-choice while 44 percent identified as pro-life.

Pro-life advocates believe that life begins when an egg is fertilized and that abortion is the murder of an unborn child. Pro-choice advocates believe that life begins when a fetus is viable, meaning it can survive outside the uterus, and that abortion should be a choice made by the individual pregnant person. A well-known slogan of the pro-choice movement is "my body, my choice." Pro-choice advocates believe that the right to choose an abortion empowers women and other people with uteruses to have control over their bodies and destinies.

abortion—a procedure that terminates a pregnancy. While many people have strong opinions on abortion, when it comes to your body, the only opinion that matters is yours. The reality is, roughly three out of ten women have an abortion at some point in their lives, according to the Guttmacher Institute. Abortion is both safe and legal, though it is difficult to obtain in some states. Having an abortion performed in a clinic or doctor's office is very safe. Fewer than 0.23 percent of women who have an abortion when they are twelve weeks pregnant or less have complications. Having an abortion is very unlikely to affect your chance of getting pregnant later, and it does not affect your risk for breast cancer.

If you are considering having an abortion, be sure to talk to a specialist about what it entails. If you have decided you want an abortion, it is best to do the procedure as soon as possible because the procedures for first-trimester abortions are less invasive.

There are a few types of abortion:

- Medication abortion, also called the abortion pill, is a pill that interrupts the pregnancy and expels the embryo from the uterus. You can take it if you are up to ten weeks pregnant, and it is more effective the sooner you take it. One benefit is that you can take this pill in the privacy of your own home.
- Vacuum aspiration, or suction aspiration, is an in-clinic abortion procedure in which the embryo is removed from the uterus by suction. You can have this procedure up until you are about fourteen to sixteen weeks pregnant. It takes ten to fifteen minutes.
- If you are more than sixteen weeks pregnant, you can have a dilation and evacuation abortion. This procedure can take up to two days and involves dilating the cervix and using tubes and surgical instruments to remove fetal tissue from the uterus.

All three types of abortion cause some physical stress. Most people feel severe cramping during and after an abortion. Many people experience flulike symptoms, including nausea, vomiting, and fever. It is

Even though abortion is legal in the United States, it is still hotly debated in many parts of the country and all over the world.

also common to bleed a fair amount after the procedure, even for up to two weeks. Listen to your doctor and follow her instructions on how to care for yourself. Emotionally, abortions can be hard. Even when you are certain you are doing the right thing, you may still feel conflicted. Feeling relieved, sad, worried, or regretful is normal. Be sure to have some emotional support around, whether it's a parent, a counselor, or a friend. No matter what, though, when it comes to having an abortion, you should not let anyone make the decision for you.

CHAPTER SIX

WHAT'S THE BIG DEAL ABOUT BIRTH CONTROL?

There's no getting around it—people have a lot of opinions about birth control. Some people believe it increases immoral behavior—an idea stemming from religious doctrines. Others believe it is the key to equality for women. Understanding other people's viewpoints is important, but when you are making decisions about your body, remember that the right decision is the one that works for you.

BIRTH CONTROL AND RELIGION

Many organized religions discourage the use of birth control because they believe that it leads to sex outside of marriage, and the Roman Catholic Church is officially opposed to birth control. Some elected officials fail to separate their private religious beliefs from policy that affects other people—as a result they regularly find ways to limit reproductive health and access to birth control and abortions. Politicians in some states have leaned on legislative loopholes to make it more difficult for people to access birth control and abortions.

Tired of the blurred lines between church and state, a group of pro-choice activists formed their own religious organization, the Satanic Temple. Realizing they would have stronger political power if they phrased their arguments in the form of religious freedoms, this group uses satire to shed light on the hypocrisy of elected officials who make policy based on religion. The group has supported women through multiple abortion-related court cases, including a 2015 case in which "Mary Doe" stated that the seventy-two-hour waiting period for an abortion in Missouri violated her religious beliefs. Spokeswoman Jex

After the Trump administration rolled back access to birth control in 2017, the ACLU filed a lawsuit against the government, saying it could not authorize discrimination against women based on religion.

Blackmore stated, "The State has essentially established a religious indoctrination program intended to push a single ideological viewpoint." The group's tenets include supporting "the eternal rebel" and "enlightened inquiry and personal freedom rather than a supernatural deity." The group uses its platform as a religion to push for the true separation of church and state.

Religion continues to affect the decisions made by people in power. In October 2017, the Trump administration made a decision to roll back access to birth control by allowing employers to refuse to provide coverage for birth control due to religious objection. As a result, the American Civil Liberties Union (ACLU) filed a lawsuit against the government because, according to ACLU senior staff attorney Brigitte Amiri, "the federal government cannot authorize discrimination against women in the name of religion."

SLUT-SHAMING AND STIGMA

Despite gains made by the feminist movement, there is still a huge double standard when it comes to sex. Boys are expected to have sex and respected if they have sex with a lot of girls, but girls are judged and called sluts, thots, or other sexist names.

Many girls even experience this type of slut-shaming from well-meaning parents and teachers, who may be trying to protect them from harassment or from getting a "bad reputation." For example, many schools have dress codes with rules that forbid girls from wearing short skirts

Sixth grader Molly Neuner challenged her school's dress code after her teachers told her and her friends that they could not wear spaghetti-strap tops to school because it was a "distraction" for boys.

or spaghetti-strap tops. Girls who wear these clothes are accused of "distracting" boys at their school. But these rules teach girls that boys aren't responsible for their own words and behavior, and that if a girl is sexually harassed, it's her own fault. By telling girls they have to change clothing so they are not distracting to their male classmates, schools are teaching girls that their learning is less important than that of their male peers.

Some girls have taken this matter into their own hands. Teenage girls at Urbana Middle School in Frederick County, Maryland, made homemade shirts saying #IAmMoreThanADistraction to protest their school's sexist dress codes.

UNDERSTANDING CONSENT

The stigma around sex leads to other kinds of damage, too. Rape culture is a term for a society in which sexual assault is normalized because of attitudes about gender and sexuality—for example, the idea that if a girl is wearing sexy clothes or if she has lots of sexual partners, then it's her own fault if she is sexually harassed or assaulted. High levels of sexual violence among young people have led activists to campaign for consent education in schools and colleges so people can learn to truly understand what consent means.

There are a few things you can do to make sure your partner really wants to have sex with you:

1. Don't assume that someone wants to have sex with you because of the way she is dressed or the way she looks at you.
2. Just because somebody had sex with you in the past, don't assume he wants to have sex with you again. Get consent every time.
3. Just because you are married to someone, it doesn't mean you have the right to have sex with her. Marital rape is a serious issue.
4. Just because a person doesn't say no, it doesn't mean she actively wants to have sex with you. If you are not sure, ask!
5. If a person is drunk, she can't give consent. Even if she wanted to have sex with you earlier in the night, don't assume she still does.

(continued on the next page)

New students at San Diego State University orientation watch a video that helps clarify the meaning of sexual consent. Schools must continue to work to educate and protect students.

(continued from the previous page)

6. Read your partner's body language. Is he excited and enthusiastic about having sex with you? Just because he doesn't say "no" or "stop," don't assume he wants to have sex.

When sex is viewed not as a shameful act but as a normal, healthy activity, it allows for honest conversations about sex and consent.

What does this have to do with birth control? If a girl feels judged or shamed for having sex, she is less likely to seek out information about birth control and less likely to use protection when she has sex. Words and actions matter, especially when it comes to sex.

THE FUTURE OF BIRTH CONTROL

Sex and stigma and birth control and pregnancy. It's a lot to navigate, especially as a teenager. It can still be scary as an adult. As your body changes, your needs might change, too. A type of birth control that worked really well in your teens may not work in your twenties.

The future of birth control relies on people making their voices heard and demanding what they need. People with uteruses shouldn't have to shoulder the burden of birth control alone. The path to better access to birth control will come from everyone working together to advocate for better education and access for all.

10 GREAT QUESTIONS TO ASK A HEALTH CARE PROVIDER

1. I don't like my current birth control. What are my options?
2. How do I talk to my parents about going on birth control?
3. What do hormones do to my body?
4. How is the IUD different from the injection or the implant?
5. I'm scared of having something in me. Are these methods safe?
6. How do I monitor my birth control to make sure it's working for me?
7. I can't talk to my partner about protection. What should I do?
8. I smoke. What birth control can I safely take?
9. Will antibiotics affect my birth control?
10. What does emergency contraception do to my body?

abortion A procedure that terminates a pregnancy.

birth control A method used to prevent a pregnancy.

chestfeed A term for breastfeeding that is sometimes used by transgender men or nonbinary people who give birth and breastfeed their babies.

cisgender A person whose biological sex matches his or her gender identity.

condom A physical barrier between two people having sex; includes external (male) condoms and internal (female) condoms.

consent Permission. Getting consent for sex is the practice of making sure the person you are about to have sex with really wants to have sex with you.

contraception Another word for birth control.

estrogen A hormone produced in the ovaries and involved in reproduction. It is also chemically mimicked in some forms of birth control to prevent pregnancy.

eugenics A set of beliefs that supports selective breeding and forcible sterilization of groups of people considered to be "undesirable."

hormones Chemical messengers that control bodily functions, such as when a body releases an egg.

intrauterine device (IUD) A small plastic device inserted into a uterus to prevent pregnancy. IUDs exist in both hormonal and nonhormonal forms.

menopause The transition that a person with ovaries makes from being fertile and having her menstrual period. It marks the end of her reproductive period.

ovulation The time when a person's body releases an egg from the ovaries during the menstrual cycle.

pro-choice A political stance that supports a pregnant person's right to choose to have an abortion; the belief that abortion should be legal.

progestin A synthetic hormone made to mimic progesterone. In birth control, progestin thickens cervical mucus to help prevent pregnancy.

pro-life A political stance based on the belief that life begins when an egg is fertilized and that abortion should be illegal.

sexual intercourse A type of sex that involves penetration with a penis.

sexually transmitted diseases (STDs) Also known as sexually transmitted infections (STIs). Diseases that are specifically contracted through sexual contact.

spermicide Chemical creams inserted into the vagina that kill sperm.

sterilization Surgery that permanently makes a person infertile; includes tubal ligation and vasectomy.

stigma A mark of disgrace or shame on a person or action, designated by cultural norms and opinions.

tubal ligation A permanent surgical form of birth control for cisgender women and other people with uteruses. The operation blocks the fallopian tubes so sperm cannot meet an egg to fertilize it.

vasectomy A permanent surgical form of birth control for cisgender men and others who produce sperm. The operation blocks sperm from entering the seminal fluid.

FOR MORE INFORMATION

American Sexual Health Association
(919) 361-8400
Website: http://www.ashasexualhealth.org
Facebook: @AmericanSexualHealthAssociation
Twitter: @InfoASHA
The American Sexual Health Association promotes the
    sexual health of individuals, families, and communities
    by advocating for sound policies and practices and
    educating the public, professionals, and policy makers
    in order to foster healthy sexual behaviors and relation-
    ships and prevent adverse health outcomes.

Bedsider
Website: https://www.bedsider.org
Facebook, Instagram, and Twitter: @Bedsider
Bedsider is an online resource for women who want to
    have sex but aren't ready for babies yet. It is full of use-
    ful information and has a casual, nonjudgmental tone.
    Bedsider has tons of resources, and it feels like you're
    talking to a friend when you read it.

Percy Skuy Collection, Dittrick Medical History Center
Case Western Reserve University
11000 Euclid Avenue
Cleveland, OH 44106
Website: http://case.edu/affil/skuyhistcontraception
    /index.html
Instagram: @dittrickmuseum

Twitter: @DittrickMuseum
This museum contains the world's most comprehensive
    collection of historical contraceptive devices, includ-
    ing more than 1,100 artifacts as well as a collection of
    historical literature on the topic of birth control.

Planned Parenthood
(800) 230-PLAN
Website: https://www.plannedparenthood.org
Facebook and Instagram: @PlannedParenthood
Twitter: @PPFA
Planned Parenthood runs more than six hundred health
    centers that offer services from STD treatments, cancer
    screenings, prenatal care, birth control, and abortions.
    Planned Parenthood also has a highly informative web-
    site with links to connect you with doctors in your area.

Public Health Agency of Canada: Sexual Health and Sex-
    ually Transmitted Infections
Website: https://www.canada.ca/en/public-health
    /services/infectious-diseases/sexual-health
    -sexually-transmitted-infections.html
Facebook: @HealthyCdns
Twitter: @GovCanHealth
Run by the Canadian government, this page has lots of
    information on STDs, how to prevent them, and what to
    do if you contract one.

Sex & U
https://www.sexandu.ca
Facebook: @sogc.org

Twitter: @SOGCorg
YouTube: sexandu
This Canadian online resource has information about sex,
STDs, pregnancy, and more. Sex and U is an initiative
of the Society of Obstetricians and Gynaecologists
of Canada.

SexEd
Website: http://sexedproject.org
Email: liz@sexedproject.org
Facebook: @S3x3dproject
SexEd is an "art-inspired community-based US sex
education" program with a mission to destigmatize sex
so as to better educate students on important issues.
It uses art in collaboration with education to spread
awareness about consent and facilitate open conver-
sations about sex.

Sexuality Information and Education Council of the United
States (SIECUS)
1012 14th Street NW, Suite 1108
Washington, DC 20005
(202) 265-2405
Email: info@siecus.org
Website: http://www.siecus.org/index.cfm
Facebook and Twitter: @siecus
SIECUS advocates for the rights of all people to be able to
obtain accurate information and comprehensive edu-
cation about sexuality and the full spectrum of sexual
and reproductive health services.

Cappiello, Katie. *Now That We're Men: The Play.* New York, NY: The Feminist Press, 2016.

Cappiello, Katie, and Meg McInerney. *Slut: A Play and Guidebook for Combating Sexism and Sexual Violence.* New York, NY: The Feminist Press, 2015.

Eig, Jonathan. *The Birth of the Pill: How Four Crusaders Reinvented Sex and Launched a Revolution.* London, England: Pan Books, 2016.

Harding, Kate. *Asking for It: The Alarming Rise of Rape Culture and What We Can Do About It.* Boston, MA: Da Capo Press, 2015.

Henderson, Elisabeth, and Nancy Armstrong. *100 Questions You'd Never Ask Your Parents: Straight Answers to Teens' Questions about Sex, Sexuality, and Health.* New York, NY: Roaring Brook Press, 2013.

Joannides, *Paul. Guide to Getting It On! A Book About the Wonders of Sex.* Waldport, OR: Goofy Foot Press, 2012.

Kambert, Mary-Lane. *Teen Pregnancy and Motherhood.* New York, NY: Rosen Publishing, 2013.

Merino, Noel. *Teen Rights and Freedoms: Birth Control.* New York, NY: Greenhaven Publishing, 2013.

Wittenstein, Vikki Oransky. *Reproductive Rights: Who Decides?* Minneapolis, MN: Lerner Publishing Group, 2016.

Wolny, Philip. *I Have an STD. Now What?* New York, NY: Rosen Publishing, 2015.

BBC News. "Trump Rolls Back Access to Free Birth Control." October 6, 2017. http://www.bbc.com/news/world-us-canada-41528526.

Beck, Julie. "The Different Stakes of Male and Female Birth Control." *Atlantic*, November 1, 2016. https://www.theatlantic.com/health/archive/2016/11/the-different-stakes-of-male-and-female-birth-control/506120.

Bedsider. "IUD – Birth Control Method." Retrieved January 6, 2018. https://www.bedsider.org/methods/iud.

Case Western Reserve University. "Anthony Comstock's Influence." Highlights of the Percy Skuy History of Contraception Gallery. Retrieved December 27, 2017. https://case.edu/affil/skuyhistcontraception/online-2012/Comstock.html.

Clearblue. "What Is Ovulation?" December 6, 2017. http://www.clearblue.com/how-to-get-pregnant/what-is-ovulation.

French, Aironius. "Birth Control Long-Term Side Effects." Livestrong, August 14, 2017. https://www.livestrong.com/article/254442-birth-control-long-term-side-effects.

Gibson, Megan. "The Long, Strange History of Birth Control." *Time*, February 2, 2015. http://time.com/3692001/birth-control-history-djerassi.

Ko, Lisa. "Unwanted Sterilization and Eugenics Programs in the United States." PBS.org, January 29, 2016. http://www.pbs.org/independentlens/blog/unwanted-sterilization-and-eugenics-programs-in-the-united-states.

Kohli, Sonali. "The Problem with Slut Shaming in Schools." *Los Angeles Times*, February 22, 2016. http://www.latimes.com/local/education/lausd/la-me-edu-slut-shaming-20160218-story.html.

Live Science. "7 Surprising Facts about The Pill." Retrieved January 9, 2018. https://www.livescience.com/14691-surprising-birth-control-pill-facts.html.

Oyez. "Body Politic: *Roe v. Wade*." Retrieved December 28, 2017. https://www.oyez.org/cases/1971/70-18.

Planned Parenthood. "Abortion After the First Trimester in the United States." February 2014. https://www.plannedparenthood.org/files/5113/9611/5527/Abortion_After_first_trimester.pdf.

Planned Parenthood. "Birth Control: Diaphragm" Retrieved January 6, 2018. https://www.plannedparenthood.org/learn/birth-control/diaphragm.

Planned Parenthood. "Birth Control Has Expanded Opportunity for Women in Economic Advancement, Educational Attainment, and Health Outcomes." June 2015. https://www.plannedparenthood.org.

Planned Parenthood. "How Effective Is the Birth Control Pill?" Retrieved January 4, 2018. https://www.plannedparenthood.org/learn/birth-control/birth-control-pill/how-effective-is-the-birth-control-pill.

Sanger, Margaret. "Morality and Birth Control." *Birth Control Review*. February–March, 1918.

Siemaszko, Corky. "Satanic Temple Challenges Missouri's Abortion Law on Religious Grounds." NBC News, January 24, 2018. https://www.nbcnews.com/news/us-news/satanic-temple-challenges-missouri-s-abortion-law-religious-grounds-n839891.

Silverman, Laura. "Mobile App Designed to Prevent Pregnancy Gets EU Approval." NPR.org, July 13, 2017. https://www.npr.org/sections/health -shots/2017/07/13/536974741/mobile-app-designed -to-prevent-pregnancy-gets-e-u-approval.

Singh, Susheela, and Jacqueline E. Dorroch. "Adding It Up: Costs and Benefits of Contraceptive Services— Estimates for 2012." Guttmacher Institute, February 25, 2016. https://www.guttmacher.org/report /adding-it-costs-and-benefits-contraceptive-services -estimates-2012.

Stanger-Hall, Kathrin F., and David W. Hall. "Absti- nence-Only Education and Teen Pregnancy Rates: Why We Need Comprehensive Sex Education in the U.S." *PLOS ONE*, October 14, 2011. http://journals .plos.org/plosone/article?id=10.1371/journal .pone.0024658.

Thompson, Kirsten M. J. "A Brief History of Birth Control in the U.S." Our Bodies Ourselves, December 14, 2013. https://www.ourbodiesourselves.org/health-info/a-brief -history-of-birth-control.

Thompson, Kirsten M. J. "Why Birth Control Is Essen- tial to Women Everywhere." Our Bodies Ourselves, December 14, 2013. https://www.ourbodiesourselves .org/health-info/why-birth-control-is-essential -to-women-everywhere.

Thorpe, J. R. "The One Thing Nobody Tells You About the IUD." Bustle, February 29, 2016. https://www.bustle com/articles/144818-the-one-thing-nobody-tells-you -about-the-copper-iud.

A

abortion, 41–44, 45–46
  back-alley, 9, 14
  death from unsafe, 14
  legality of, 12, 14, 42
abstinence, 37–38
American Civil Liberties Union
  (ACLU), 47
Amiri, Brigitte, 47

B

birth control
  in ancient times, 7
  effectiveness of, 15, 19, 20,
    22, 29–30
  global access to, 13–14
  hormonal, 16–24
  legal challenges, 8
  legalization of, 10, 11–12
  natural methods, 32–38
  nonhormonal, 25–31
  opposition to, 8
  and religion, 45–47
  side effects, 17–18, 21–22,
    23–24, 26, 36, 41
  and STDs, 15, 24, 26–27, 31
birth control pill (the Pill), 18–19
  effectiveness, 19, 34
  for men, 36

research for first-ever,
  10–11
safety of, 12
two types of, 18–19

C

cervical caps, 28–30
Comstock, Anthony, 8–10
Comstock Act of 1973, 9
condoms, 26–28
consent education, 49–51

D

diaphragms, 28–30
dress codes, 47–48

E

Eig, Jonathan, 7
emergency contraception,
  40–44
estrogen, 18, 19

F

fallopian tubes, 16, 31
family planning, 13–14
fertility tracking, 32–34
forced sterilization, 29